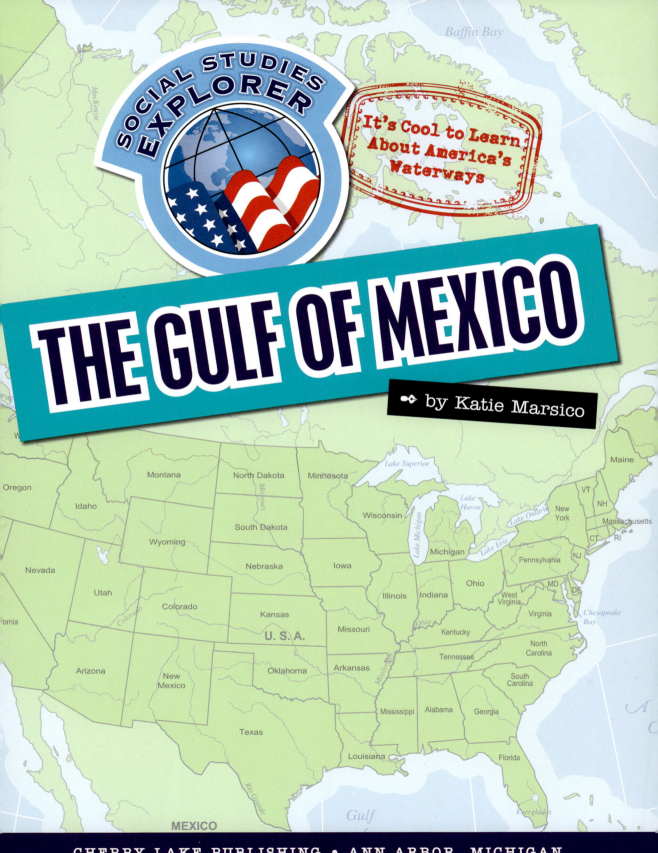

Published in the United States of America
by Cherry Lake Publishing
Ann Arbor, Michigan
www.cherrylakepublishing.com

Content Adviser: James Wolfinger, PhD, Associate Professor,
History and Teacher Education, DePaul University, Chicago, Illinois

Book Design: The Design Lab

Photo Credits: Cover and page 3, ©Bill Ragan/Shutterstock, Inc., ©Brian
Lasenby/Shutterstock, Inc., ©Steven Frame/Dreamstime.com, ©Daniel
Korzeniewski/Shutterstock, Inc., ©Neftali/Shutterstock, Inc.; back cover
and page 3, ©rj lerich/Shutterstock, Inc.; page 4, ©Nagel Photography/
Shutterstock, Inc.; page 6, ©Lucy Clark/Shutterstock, Inc.; page 9, ©Brian
Lasenby/Shutterstock, Inc.; page 11, ©Steven Frame/Shutterstock,
Inc.; page 12, AP Photo/Derick E. Hingle; page 13, ©UgputuLf SS/
Shutterstock, Inc.; page 14, ©AP Photo/Marcio Jose Sanchez; page 17,
©Antonio Abrignani/Shutterstock, Inc.; page 18, ©Richard Goldberg/
Shutterstock, Inc.; page 20, ©Jaimie Duplass/Shutterstock, Inc.; page
21, ©Philip Lange/Shutterstock, Inc.; page 22, ©MSPhotographic/
Shutterstock, Inc.; page 23, ©Chas/Shutterstock, Inc.; page 26, ©Danny E
Hooks/Shutterstock, Inc.; page 27, ©AP Photo/NASA; page 29, ©Marcia
Crayton/Shutterstock, Inc.

Library of Congress Cataloging-in-Publication Data
Marsico, Katie, 1980–
   The Gulf of Mexico / by Katie Marsico.
      p. cm. — (It's cool to learn about America's waterways)
   Includes bibliographical references and index.
   ISBN 978-1-62431-016-4 (lib. bdg.) — ISBN 978-1-62431-040-9
(pbk.) — ISBN 978-1-62431-064-5 (e-book) 1. Mexico, Gulf of—Juvenile
literature. I. Title.

   F296.M116 2013
   551.46'1364—dc23
2012034739

Cherry Lake Publishing would like to acknowledge the work
of The Partnership for 21st Century Skills. Please visit
www.21stcenturyskills.org for more information.

Printed in the United States of America
Corporate Graphics Inc.
January 2013
CLSP12

THE GULF OF MEXICO

TABLE OF CONTENTS

Coral Reefs USA 15c
Elkhorn Coral: Florida

CHAPTER ONE

WELCOME TO THE GULF OF MEXICO!

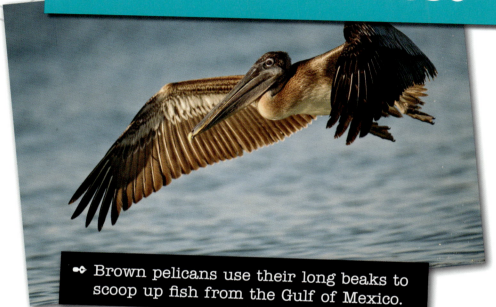

❖ Brown pelicans use their long beaks to scoop up fish from the Gulf of Mexico.

Are you excited about exploring the Gulf of Mexico? When you visit this ocean **basin**, you'll have the chance to collect seashells, splash in the surf, and enjoy a picnic underneath the shade of a palm tree. Be sure to keep your eyes peeled for local wildlife, too! Bottlenose dolphins, brown pelicans, and nurse sharks are just a few of the animals that live in Gulf Coast **habitats**.

During your adventure, you'll also learn about the history, culture, and **cuisine** connected to this incredible

waterway. (And if you like eating shrimp, you'll love dining along the Gulf of Mexico!) Seafood will shape only part of your journey. By the time you leave the gulf, you will understand the importance of protecting one of America's greatest national treasures.

A narrow waterway known as the Florida Straits links the Gulf of Mexico to the Atlantic Ocean. The Yucatan Channel—which flows between Mexico and Cuba—connects the gulf to the Caribbean Sea. The Gulf of Mexico is the ninth-largest body of water in the world. It covers approximately 617,763 square miles (1.6 million square kilometers).

Do you feel like going for a swim in the Gulf of Mexico? The average depth of this waterway is 5,300 feet (1,615 meters). If you were diving in the deepest part of the gulf, you would have to travel approximately 14,000 feet (4,267 m) to reach its floor! But you might not need your water wings. Most coastal areas feature long, narrow ridges of sand called sandbars, where the gulf is usually only a few feet deep.

➥ You can enjoy gorgeous Gulf of Mexico sunrises along the coastlines of three different countries.

Three different countries surround the Gulf of Mexico. Cuba lies to its southeast. Five Mexican states border the gulf to the southwest and west. Portions of the U.S. states Florida, Alabama, Mississippi, Louisiana, and Texas are located to the north. Together they make up the area commonly known as the Gulf Coast. Thirty-three major U.S. river systems—including the Mississippi River—empty into the gulf. Some 207 **estuaries** flow into it, too.

Your adventure will mainly focus on American shores. Be prepared to move at a quick pace, though! The Gulf of Mexico forms roughly 1,600 miles (2,575 km) of U.S. coastline. So you still have a lot of ground to cover.

ACTIVITY

STOP
Don't write in
this book!

THE GULF
OF MEXICO

GULF OF MEXICO MAP

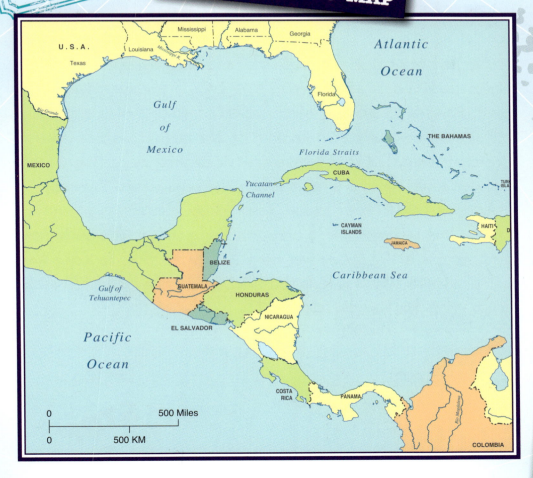

Take a close look at this map of the Gulf of Mexico. Then place a separate piece of paper over it and trace the outline of the gulf. Use a crayon or marker to shade in any U.S. states found along the Gulf Coast. Label the Florida Straits, the Atlantic Ocean, the Yucatan Channel, the Caribbean Sea, Cuba, and Mexico, too! Feel free to mark your map with other important locations you learn about in the pages ahead.

ACTIVITY

You've just read that five U.S. states bordering the Gulf of Mexico form about 1,600 miles (2,575 km) of the waterway's coast. Roughly 23 percent of the coast is along Texas. Louisiana contains approximately 24 percent of the gulf's coastline. Almost 3 percent is located in Mississippi, while slightly more than 3 percent makes up Alabama's geography. The remaining 47 percent of America's Gulf Coast is found in Florida.

Use this information to create a bar graph to illustrate how the coastline is divided among the U.S. states that lie along the Gulf of Mexico. Which bar do you think will be the longest? Which do you predict will be the shortest?

STOP Don't write in this book!

What do you think you should pack for your trip to the Gulf of Mexico? Swimwear is an absolute must. Yet keep in mind that you will not just be touring endless stretches of beach. The gulf forms the basis of more than 5 million acres (2 million hectares) of coastal wetlands in the United States alone. As you will soon discover, a rich variety of habitats exist within this **ecosystem**.

Portions of the Gulf Coast are made up of wetland prairies and hilly evergreen and pine forests. Though the gulf itself contains saltwater, nearby habitats feature freshwater swamps, marshes, lakes, rivers, and springs. You probably won't be surprised to read that the Gulf of Mexico is also the site of several different **marine** environments. These include **mangroves**, estuaries and bays, **barrier islands**, and coral reefs.

↠ Colorful coral reefs are found along the Gulf Coast.

Want to feel like you're stepping into a warm bath? Take a dip in the Gulf of Mexico! Depending on the exact location and the time of year, water temperatures sometimes climb as high as 87 degrees Fahrenheit (30.6 degrees Celsius)! During winter months, they usually don't fall much lower than 51°F (10.6°C).

Luckily, no matter which of these habitats you explore, you can leave any bulky sweaters and winter coats at home. That's because the Gulf Coast has a semitropical climate. In other words, you'll likely experience humid, warm weather.

Gulf Coast summers can get quite hot. But you'll find that gentle sea breezes blow off the water and often help cool things down. Winters are generally mild, and frost and snow are unusual. This is not true of rain, however, so you should probably bring an umbrella with you. In the summer of 2012, several U.S. communities located along the Gulf of Mexico received up to 2 feet (0.6 m) of rainfall. The gulf's hurricane season lasts from early June to late November.

A hurricane is a powerful tropical storm. It slams the coast with heavy rain and extremely destructive winds.

It's important that you are aware of the dangerous weather patterns that sometimes impact the Gulf of Mexico. Don't be too concerned, though. Sunshine makes up just as big a part of the waterway's climate as storms do. Saint Petersburg—a city on Florida's Gulf Coast—broke world records for having 768 sunny days in a row! Before you spend all your money on sunglasses, however, think about buying a camera. How else do you plan on snapping photos of the incredible wildlife you're going to read about in the next chapter?

◆➤ Saint Petersburg, Florida, is famous for its pleasant, sunny weather.

CHAPTER TWO

THE WATERWAY'S WILDLIFE

➥ Dolphins are among the many animals that depend on the Gulf of Mexico for survival.

You're almost ready to begin your Gulf of Mexico adventure. First, you should go through a checklist of the items in your suitcase. Camera? Check! Binoculars? Check! Microscope? Well . . . perhaps that's taking things too far. You may be asking why you need to pack one, since you're not planning to conduct scientific research. The answer is that you'll be observing more than 15,000 species of wildlife that exist in the gulf!

Several different kinds of sea and marsh grasses grow in or along this waterway. The Gulf of Mexico is also known for its brown, green, and red algae. These simple plants—which do not have flowers, leaves, stems, or roots—are almost always found in the water. Some species of algae are so tiny that you need a microscope to view them. Others stretch more than 200 feet (61 m) long.

You may get a chance to see algae up close when you swim in the Gulf of Mexico. Just search the waves for seaweed! Plan on taking a picture of the large clumps of sargassum, or brown algae, which frequently float across the surface of the water. But make sure your camera stays dry! Remember that you also need to capture a few scenic shots of the Gulf Coast's tangled man-groves and towering cabbage palms.

●◆ Algae frequently grow along rocky areas of the Gulf Coast.

● Fishers catch a lot of seafood—including shrimp—in the Gulf of Mexico.

Do you own swim goggles? If not, consider buying or borrowing a pair before you head to the Gulf of Mexico. Goggles will help you get a better look at some of the amazing animals that exist within this waterway!

Clams, oysters, and scallops are found in the gulf. So are corals, shrimp, lobsters, and crabs. If you carefully examine certain Gulf Coast seashells, you may discover a hermit crab or a **mollusk** living inside!

Plan on replacing your goggles with binoculars to view the 28 different kinds of dolphins, porpoises, and whales that surface above the waves to breathe air. Scientists recently estimated that there are about 45,000 bottlenose dolphins living in the Gulf of Mexico. If you're lucky, you might spot

Make Your Very Own Field Guide

How do you plan on keeping track of all the plants and animals in and along the Gulf of Mexico? You will find that a field guide often comes in handy! A field guide is a book that describes the different species found within a certain environment. Don't worry about buying a field guide before you head to the gulf. You can create your own! First, pick 20 local species (or more if you want). Write the name of each one on a separate sheet of paper. Then get ready to do some detective work on the computer or at the library. Research and record the following information for the plants and animals you have selected:

Type of plant/animal
  (tree, shrub, flower/reptile, mammal, fish):
Habitat:
Appearance:
Other interesting facts:

    After you're done, you can either print out or draw pictures of the species in your guidebook. Finally, decorate a cover and staple your pages together (or snap them into a binder). Remember to pack your field guide before you begin your adventure in the gulf!

these graceful marine mammals playing a few yards from shore. The gulf is also home to five species of sea turtles and 49 species of sharks. Countless types of birds—including brown pelicans, laughing gulls, sandwich terns, and Wilson's plovers—nest along this waterway.

Don't forget that the Gulf Coast's ecosystem is made up of more than just beaches. Species such as the Florida black bear, American alligator, and West Indian manatee live in the region's pine forests, freshwater marshes, and mangrove swamps. If you want to catch a glimpse of this wide variety of wildlife, there's no time to waste. Because you obviously have a lot to see and do, zip up your suitcase and journey forward!

Stingrays are one of countless types of fish that live in the Gulf of Mexico. They have flat, diamond-shaped bodies, and use their **barbed** tails to defend themselves. Because they often burrow in sandy areas along the ocean floor, you should plan on shuffling or wiggling your feet as you enter the water. This motion warns stingrays to move out of your path to avoid getting stepped on. It also prevents you from possibly receiving a nasty leg wound!

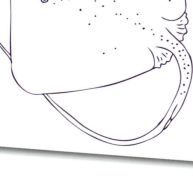

CHAPTER THREE

CHAPTER THREE

PAST AND PRESENT

➥ From American Indians to European explorers (whose ships are shown here), several groups helped shape modern Gulf Coast culture.

You're finally on your way to the Gulf of Mexico! Before you arrive, however, you need to go on a little side trip. So, close your eyes, take a deep breath, and travel back in time—300 million years, to be exact. That's when various pieces of the earth's surface shifted and caused part of the seafloor to sink. The basin that formed as a result of this movement later became the Gulf of Mexico.

Early peoples probably began living along what is now the Gulf Coast several thousand years ago. American Indians hunted, fished, and built villages there. Then, in the late

1400s, Europeans started exploring the Gulf of Mexico. The French and Spanish controlled much of this waterway and the areas surrounding it during the next few centuries.

Between 1803 and 1836, the United States acquired territories that include America's present-day Gulf Coast. U.S. merchants shipped goods and conducted trade from port cities along the gulf, including New Orleans, Louisiana, and Houston, Texas. Oil production, fishing, tourism, and farming became important to the local **economy** as well.

More than 14 million people currently live along the Gulf Coast in cities such as Tampa, Florida; Mobile, Alabama; and Gulfport-Biloxi, Mississippi.

◆ Oil rigs in the Gulf of Mexico are an important source of fuel.

TEST YOUR KNOWLEDGE

Are you an expert when it comes to Gulf Coast history? Test how much you know about the Gulf of Mexico by taking the simple quiz below. On the left side of this activity, you will see the names of five people who are linked to the gulf. On the right side, you will see the reasons these men and women are famous. Try to match each person with the correct description.

1) Amerigo Vespucci

A) Seminole leader who led his people in armed conflict against U.S. troops who had been ordered to remove the Seminoles from their land along the Gulf Coast

2) Jean Lafitte

B) American baseball legend born in the Gulf Coast region who is famous for his record number of home runs

3) Osceola

C) U.S. author whose writing often describes life and culture along Louisiana's Gulf Coast

4) Kate Chopin

D) Italian mapmaker who was probably one of the first Europeans to explore the Gulf of Mexico

5) Hank Aaron

E) French pirate in the Gulf of Mexico who aided U.S. forces fighting the British during the War of 1812

Answers: 1) D; 2) E; 3) A; 4) C; 5) B

Many different groups of people have made America's Gulf Coast the exciting, colorful region you are exploring today. For example, much of the spicy cuisine and lively folk music found throughout the area reflect Cajun culture. Cajun Americans trace their roots back to 18th-century French Canadians who settled in Louisiana. Creoles have also influenced several areas that lie along the Gulf of Mexico. Members of this group usually have a combination of French, African, Spanish, and American Indian ancestry. Various American Indian nations and people from Mexico and the Caribbean have also shaped local culture.

Now that you've learned a little bit about the background of the gulf, you can officially begin your adventure! Where do you want to go first? Sanibel Island, Florida, and Gulf Islands National Seashore in Mississippi are perfect for swimming and collecting shells. Think about doing some kayaking and snorkeling there as well. Or, if you're feeling tired, you can always kick back and relax aboard a boat in Orange Beach,

Alabama. Visitors to Orange Beach often take special cruises that tour areas in the gulf where bottlenose dolphins are frequently sighted.

Perhaps you'd prefer to visit a floating museum instead? If so, head to Corpus Christi Bay in Texas! You'll be able to explore "Lex," a former World War II (1939–1945) aircraft carrier. This ship now sits in the gulf and serves as the USS Lexington Museum. While you're in Texas, try to check out Port Isabel. The lighthouse there guided boats along the Gulf Coast as far back as the 1850s.

●○ Visitors aboard the USS *Lexington* have the opportunity to learn more about World War II.

Has all this traveling worked up your appetite? You'll find that many Gulf Coast restaurants offer fresh seafood, including lobster, crab, shrimp, and oysters. Spicy Cajun dishes such as jambalaya and gumbo are also popular along the gulf. Jambalaya is made from rice, tomatoes, peppers, onions, and celery. Either ham, sausage, chicken, or shellfish is mixed in. Gumbo is a thick soup or stew. It's usually prepared with either chicken or seafood and a vegetable called okra.

Don't be surprised if you see conch listed as an ingredient on Gulf Coast menus. A conch is a tropical marine mollusk. Conch meat is frequently used in salads and rich soups called chowders.

➻ Gumbo is often seasoned with spicy peppers.

⚬ Pecan pie is a popular sweet treat in areas along the Gulf Coast.

For dessert, help yourself to a serving of either pecan pie or key lime pie. If you have an especially sweet tooth, sample some pralines. These crisp cookie-size candies are made with brown sugar, butter, and pecans.

After dinner, think about taking a stroll on the sand. Or you can walk along one of the many boardwalks that stretch along the shore. Another option is to check out a local festival or fair. If you happen to visit Louisiana's Gulf Coast in spring, stop by the New Orleans Jazz & Heritage Festival. While you're there, you'll hear everything from rhythm and blues to rock 'n' roll to **zydeco**!

Before long, it will be time for you to bring your adventure in the Gulf of Mexico to a close. But first, you'll have to tie up a few loose ends. Keep reading to learn what you can and should do to help protect this remarkable American waterway.

ACTIVITY RECIPE

Coconut shrimp is a popular treat at some Gulf Coast restaurants. You can prepare this seafood dish at home, too. Just remember to have an adult help you clean the shrimp and operate the oven!

Baked Coconut Shrimp

INGREDIENTS
Cooking spray
1 pound large shrimp
1/3 cup cornstarch
1 teaspoon salt
3/4 teaspoon cayenne pepper
2 cups flaked, sweetened coconut
Three egg whites

INSTRUCTIONS

1. Coat a baking sheet with cooking spray and preheat your oven to 400°F (200°C).

2. Rinse the shrimp under cold water and pat them dry with a paper towel. (Be sure to ask an adult to help you remove any of the tiny veins that are often found on fresh shrimp!)

3. Mix the cornstarch, salt, and cayenne pepper together in a bowl. Put the coconut flakes in a second bowl.

4. In a third bowl, beat the egg whites until they are slightly foamy.

5. Pick up a cleaned shrimp and dip it deep into your cornstarch mixture. Next, soak the shrimp in egg whites. Finally, roll the shrimp in coconut flakes until it is completely coated. Then place it on your baking sheet. Repeat these steps with each individual shrimp.

6. After the oven has finished preheating, place the baking sheet inside. Bake the shrimp for roughly 7 to 10 minutes. Then flip them, and bake for another 7 to 10 minutes. (You'll be able to tell that the shrimp are done when they are bright pink on the outside and the coconut batter is browned.)

7. Turn off the oven and carefully remove your baking sheet. Let the shrimp cool for a few minutes before treating yourself to a taste of the gulf!

CHAPTER FOUR

TAKING CARE OF A NATIONAL TREASURE

➤ Thick black oil coated Gulf Coast beaches following the Deepwater Horizon disaster.

Do you remember any recent news stories about the Gulf of Mexico? This waterway made headlines in April 2010. That was when an oil well called Deepwater Horizon exploded in the gulf. For three months, more than 190 million gallons (719 million liters) of oil spilled into the water and onto the coast. The leak injured and killed countless plants and animals and destroyed the habitats of many others. Have you

seen any photographs or video footage of how gulf species were affected? You may have felt sad, angry, and helpless. Fortunately, Americans just like you can take steps to prevent similar tragedies from occurring in the future.

Human activity has threatened or endangered more than 400 species of plants and animals in the gulf. Endangered species are at risk of being wiped off the earth. Threatened species are likely to face such a risk in the near future.

Events such as the 2010 oil spill represent only one threat to the gulf. Water pollution and the clearing of coastal areas for development are others. Overfishing and certain types of fishing equipment are also harmful to local wildlife.

As you complete your journey, steer clear of the gulf's Dead Zone! This portion of the Gulf of Mexico, off the coast of Louisiana, has extremely low oxygen levels. Many plants and animals are unable to exist there. Pollution is the main factor affecting the Dead Zone. The size of this area changes from year to year. In 2012, scientists estimated that the gulf's Dead Zone measured up to 6,200 square miles (16,058 sq km).

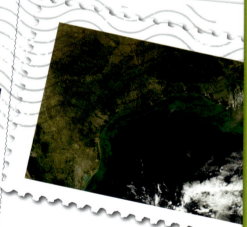

ACTIVITY

WRITE A LETTER

Political leaders in Texas, Louisiana, Mississippi, Alabama, and Florida have the power to shape the future of the Gulf of Mexico. Along with other politicians across the country, these men and women make important decisions about laws and government projects that protect America's waterways. Writing a letter to such individuals lets them know that people like you care about the gulf. Ask an adult to help you find the addresses of officials involved in Gulf Coast **conservation** efforts. Then create a short, simple letter using the following outline:

Dear [INSERT THE NAME OF THE POLITICIAN(S) YOU DECIDE TO WRITE TO]:

I am writing to ask for your help in protecting the Gulf of Mexico. The Gulf Coast is important to me because [INSERT TWO OR THREE REASONS THE GULF MATTERS TO YOU].

Thanks for your efforts to support this amazing American waterway!

Sincerely,

[INSERT YOUR NAME]

Luckily, a growing number of scientists and government leaders are working with U.S. citizens of all ages to encourage conservation efforts in the Gulf of Mexico. Many Americans cleaned up beaches and other nearby habitats after the 2010 oil spill. They cared for sick and injured wildlife. They also relocated animals to protected areas in or along the gulf.

Sometimes conservation is as simple as sharing information. Talk to your family and friends about all that you have experienced during your trip to the Gulf of Mexico. Remember, it's up to you to spread the word about this American waterway. It is truly an amazing and irreplaceable national treasure!

◗ With your help, the Gulf of Mexico will remain one of America's most beautiful natural treasures for years to come.

GLOSSARY

barbed (BARBD) having a sharp point that sticks outward and backward

barrier islands (BAR-ee-ur EYE-luhndz) long, narrow, sandy islands that run parallel to a coastal mainland

basin (BAY-suhn) an area of land drained by a river system

conservation (kahn-sur-VAY-shuhn) the protection of valuable things, especially wildlife, natural resources, forests, or artistic or historic objects

cuisine (kwi-ZEEN) a style or manner of cooking or presenting food

economy (i-KAH-nuh-mee) the system of buying, selling, making things, and managing money in a place

ecosystem (EE-koh-sis-tuhm) all the livings things in a place and their relation to the environment

estuaries (ES-choo-er-eez) arms of the sea that meet the mouth of a river

habitats (HAB-uh-tats) places where an animal or a plant naturally lives

mangroves (MAN-grohvz) trees or shrubs that grow in saltwater and have roots that rise into the air

marine (muh-REEN) of or having to do with the ocean

mollusk (MAH-luhsk) an animal with a soft body, no spine, and usually a hard shell that lives in water or a damp habitat

zydeco (ZYE-duh-ko) music of southern Louisiana that combines tunes of French origin with elements of Caribbean music and the blues, and that features guitar, washboard, and accordion

FOR MORE INFORMATION

BOOKS

Bouler, Olivia. *Olivia's Birds: Saving the Gulf.* New York: Sterling Publishing, 2011.

Landau, Elaine. *Oil Spill! Disaster in the Gulf of Mexico.* Minneapolis: Millbrook Press, 2011.

WEB SITES

Gulf of Mexico Foundation—Kids and Students
www.gulfmex.org/archive/kids.htm
This site features links to online videos, games, and kids' blogs that focus on Gulf Coast conservation efforts.

National Wildlife Federation—The Big Oil Spill
http://www.nwf.org/Kids/Ranger-Rick/People-and-Places/Ranger-Rick-on-The-Big-Oil-Spill.aspx
This Web site includes Ranger Rick's answers to common questions about the 2010 oil spill in the Gulf of Mexico.

ABOUT THE AUTHOR
Katie Marsico has written more than 100 books for young readers. The Gulf of Mexico is her favorite American waterway, and she vacations there as often as possible. Ms. Marsico dedicates this book to her daughter and faithful traveling companion, Maria.